WE'RE RIGHT BEHIND YOU, CHARLIE BROWN

Weekly Reader Books presents

WE'RE RIGHT BEHIND YOU,
CHARLIE BROWN

A NEW PEANUTS BOOK

by Charles M. Schulz

HOLT, RINEHART AND WINSTON

New York · Chicago · San Francisco

Published simultaneously in Canada by Holt, Rinehart
and Winston of Canada, Limited.

Library of Congress Catalog Card Number: 63-20880

ISBN: 0–03–042990–0

Printed in the United States of America

WHATEVER HAPPENED TO THE GOOD OLD-FASHIONED NEIGHBORHOOD DOG?

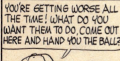

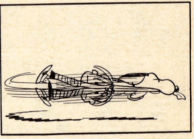

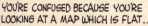

PTUI!

PTUI!

UNTIL IT IS DEMONSTRATED, ONE FORGETS THE REALLY GREAT DIFFERENCE THAT EXISTS BETWEEN THE MERELY COMPETENT AMATEUR AND THE VERY EXPERT PROFESSIONAL

WHAT ARE WE WATCHING?

WELL, FOR ONCE WE'RE WATCHING WHAT **I** WANNA WATCH!

I GOT THE TV FIRST SO WE'RE GONNA WATCH **MY** PROGRAM!

ALL RIGHT! ALL RIGHT! I'M NOT SAYING A WORD!

CAN YOU SEE SITTING WAY BACK THERE? HOW ABOUT THE VOLUME? IS IT LOUD ENOUGH?

WHY DON'T I JUST TRY TO GET THE PICTURE A LITTLE CLEARER.... I THINK IT NEEDS MORE CONTRAST..

WHY DON'T YOU MOVE UP CLOSER? A RECENT OPHTHALMOLOGIST'S REPORT SAID THAT IT'S ALL RIGHT TO SIT UP CLOSE...

THIS IS A GOOD PROGRAM...YOU WERE SMART TO WANT TO WATCH THIS PROGRAM.. IT'S VERY GOOD...

WHY DON'T I MOVE THE AERIAL A LITTLE? I THINK WE CAN GET A BETTER PICTURE IF I JIGGLE IT JUST A LITTLE..

HOW ABOUT THE SOUND NOW? IS IT TOO LOUD OR IS IT JUST ABOUT THE WAY YOU LIKE IT? IF YOU'D LIKE, I CAN...

ALL RIGHT! I GIVE UP! YOU CAN WATCH YOUR OWN PROGRAM!

DO YOU MEAN IT?

SURE, I MEAN IT! GO AHEAD...CHANGE THE CHANNEL...

GOOD!

SCHULZ

NOW, LOOK...THIS IS **MY** PROGRAM WE'RE GONNA WATCH SO LET'S HAVE IT QUIET IN HERE! NO TALKING! UNDERSTAND?!!

SIGH

EXCUSE ME...

CLOMP!

THANK YOU VERY MUCH..

THINK NOTHING OF IT...YOU'LL HEAR FROM THE HUMANE SOCIETY FIRST THING IN THE MORNING!

HEY, WAKE UP...IT'S ALMOST THERE!

WHAM!

FOR A SEVEN-TEN SPLIT HE WAKES ME UP!

SCHULZ

PHOOEY!

WHAT'S THE MATTER?

MY LIFE IS A DRAG... I'M COMPLETELY FED UP.. I'VE NEVER FELT SO LOW IN MY LIFE...

WHEN YOU'RE IN A MOOD LIKE THIS YOU SHOULD TRY TO THINK OF THINGS YOU HAVE TO BE THANKFUL FOR...IN OTHER WORDS, COUNT YOUR BLESSINGS.

HA! THAT'S A GOOD ONE! I COULD COUNT MY BLESSINGS ON ONE FINGER! I'VE NEVER **HAD** ANYTHING, AND I NEVER **WILL** HAVE ANYTHING!

I DON'T GET HALF THE BREAKS THAT OTHER PEOPLE DO...NOTHING EVER GOES RIGHT FOR ME!

AND YOU TALK ABOUT COUNTING BLESSINGS! YOU TALK ABOUT BEING THANKFUL! WHAT DO **I** HAVE TO BE THANKFUL FOR?

WELL, FOR ONE THING, YOU HAVE A LITTLE BROTHER WHO LOVES YOU...

WAAH!

EVERY NOW AND THEN I SAY THE RIGHT THING..

SCHULZ

IT'S KIND OF COLD TONIGHT...IT SHOULDN'T BE SO COLD THIS TIME OF YEAR...

I WONDER IF SNOOPY IS WARM ENOUGH...

I THINK I'LL TAKE MY SLEEPING BAG OUT TO HIM..

IF A PERSON IS GOING TO OWN A DOG, HE MUST LEARN TO ASSUME THE OBLIGATIONS OF THAT OWNERSHIP!

I'M GLAD I TOOK IT OUT TO HIM..HE SEEMED TO APPRECIATE IT..

I CAN SLEEP BETTER MYSELF NOW, KNOWING THAT HE'S WARM..

THERE'S NEVER ANYTHING TO DO!

I NEED SOMETHING TO CHALLENGE ME.. I NEED SOME NEW INTEREST...

IF YOU WANT A HOBBY, WHY DON'T YOU COLLECT LEAVES? YOU CAN PRESS THEM BETWEEN THE PAGES OF A BOOK..

THAT'S A WONDERFUL IDEA!

WHAP!

WELL, I DID IT! I'VE COLLECTED OVER A DOZEN DIFFERENT KINDS OF LEAVES!

MY ONLY PROBLEM CAME IN SELECTING WHAT SORT OF BOOK I SHOULD PRESS THEM IN..OF COURSE, I KNEW IT HAD TO BE A LARGE VOLUME...

I FIRST THOUGHT OF "THE DECLINE AND FALL OF THE ROMAN EMPIRE," AND THEN I CONSIDERED "LOOK HOMEWARD ANGEL," BUT I FINALLY DECIDED ON A VOLUME CALLED, "THE PROPHECIES OF DANIEL" BECAUSE I FELT THAT..

GET OUT OF HERE!

PEOPLE REALLY AREN'T INTERESTED IN HEARING YOU TALK ABOUT YOUR HOBBY..

SCHULZ

YOU NEVER KNOW IN WHICH PART OF THE COUNTRY IT WILL HAPPEN..

ON HALLOWEEN NIGHT IN 1959 THE GREAT PUMPKIN APPEARED IN THE PUMPKIN PATCH OF BOOTS RUTMAN OF CONNECTICUT..

IF YOU DON'T BELIEVE ME, LOOK IN THE RECORD!

IN 1960 THE GREAT PUMPKIN APPEARED IN THE PUMPKIN PATCH OF R.W. DANIELS OF TEXAS...

AGAIN I SAY, IF YOU DON'T BELIEVE ME, LOOK IN THE RECORD!

NOW, SOMEWHERE IN THIS WORLD THE GREAT PUMPKIN HAS TO APPEAR THIS HALLOWEEN NIGHT!

WHY NOT HERE?!

MAYBE THIS PUMPKIN PATCH ISN'T BIG ENOUGH?

SIZE HAS NOTHING TO DO WITH IT! IT'S SINCERITY THAT COUNTS! ASK BOOTS RUTMAN! ASK R.W. DANIELS!

MAYBE IT'S NEATNESS, TOO...MAYBE HE APPEARS IN THE PUMPKIN PATCH THAT HAS THE LEAST WEEDS

NO, NO, NO, NO, NO, NO, NO! IT'S SINCERITY THAT COUNTS! THE GREAT PUMPKIN WILL APPEAR IN WHICHEVER PUMPKIN PATCH HE DECIDES IS THE MOST SINCERE!!

I'D HATE TO HAVE TO MAKE SUCH A DECISION!

RATS! RAINY DAYS DRIVE ME CRAZY!

HEY! COME HERE!

WHAT'S UP?

THIS, LINUS, IS WHAT IS KNOWN AS A "FLANNELGRAPH"...

I HAVE TACKED A PIECE OF FLANNEL TO THIS BOARD AS YOU CAN SEE...NOW, I HAVE ALSO USED A PIECE OF FLANNEL FOR THESE LITTLE CUT-OUT FIGURES...

SEE? THE FIGURES STICK TO THE BOARD MAKING IT AN IDEAL METHOD FOR TELLING ILLUSTRATED STORIES...

NOW, IF YOU'LL JUST SIT OVER THERE, I'LL ENTERTAIN YOU WITH AN EXCITING TALE

THIS IS GREAT! WHAT INGENUITY SHE HAS!

NOW, THIS IS THE STORY OF THE SHEPHERD AND HIS THREE SHEEP... ONE DAY A SHEPHERD WAS STANDING ON A HILL...

I WONDER HOW SHE THINKS OF THINGS LIKE THIS? A FLANNELGRAPH! JUST IMAGINE!

I WONDER WHERE SHE GOT THE FLANNEL IN THE FIRST PLACE TO....

MY BLANKET!!

SCHULZ

IT SNOWED LAST NIGHT..I CAN TELL!

HOW DISGUSTING! I GO TO SLEEP AT NIGHT, AND WHEN I WAKE UP, WINTER HAS COME!

NOW I WON'T BE ABLE TO FIND MY DOG DISH OR ANYTHING! RATS! WHAT DOES IT HAVE TO SNOW FOR?!

AT LEAST I **THINK** THIS IS SNOW...I CAN'T SEE... MAYBE THERE'S SOMETHING WRONG WITH MY EYES!!

MAYBE I WENT BLIND DURING THE NIGHT! MAYBE I...

AH! SNOW! SNOW! BEAUTIFUL SNOW!!

GOOD GRIEF! A FROZEN WASTELAND!

WHERE **IS** EVERYBODY?!

THEY'VE ALL GONE! I'M ALONE! THEY'VE LEFT ME!!

I'VE BEEN LEFT ALONE TO STARVE TO DEATH! TO FREEZE TO DEATH! TO ...

YAHOO!!

ZOOM!

♥-SMACK-♥

MMMMMMM

I THINK THE DAY WILL COME WHEN THAT DOG CRACKS UP COMPLETELY!

SCHULZ

SIGH!

I DON'T THINK I'D MIND SCHOOL AT ALL IF IT WEREN'T FOR THESE LUNCH HOURS...I GUESS I'LL SIT ON THIS BENCH...

I HAVE TO SIT BY MYSELF BECAUSE NOBODY ELSE EVER INVITES ME TO SIT WITH THEM...

PEANUT BUTTER AGAIN! OH, WELL, MOM DOES HER BEST...

THOSE KIDS LOOK LIKE THEY'RE HAVING A LOT OF FUN...I WISH THEY LIKED ME... NOBODY LIKES ME...

THE PTA DID A GOOD JOB PAINTING THESE BENCHES...

I'D GIVE ANYTHING IN THE WORLD IF THAT LITTLE GIRL WITH THE RED HAIR WOULD COME OVER, AND SIT WITH ME..

I GET TIRED OF ALWAYS BEING ALONE...I WISH THE BELL WOULD RING...

A BANANA...RATS! MOM ALWAYS...STILL, I GUESS SHE MEANS WELL...

I BET I COULD RUN JUST AS FAST AS THOSE KIDS.. THAT'S A GOOD GAME THEY'RE PLAYING...

THAT LITTLE GIRL WITH THE RED HAIR IS A GOOD RUNNER...

AH, THERE'S THE BELL! ONE MORE LUNCH HOUR OUT OF THE WAY...

TWO-THOUSAND, ONE-HUNDRED AND TWENTY TO GO!

SCHULZ

I GOT IT!

YOU GIMME BACK MY BLANKET!

NO! I'VE GOT IT, AND I'M GOING TO KEEP IT! THIS IS THE START YOU NEED TO BREAK THE HABIT!

APPARENTLY YOU HAVEN'T READ THE LATEST SCIENTIFIC REPORTS..

A BLANKET IS AS IMPORTANT TO A CHILD AS A HOBBY IS TO AN ADULT..

MANY A MAN SPENDS HIS TIME RESTORING ANTIQUE AUTOMOBILES OR BUILDING MODEL TRAINS OR COLLECTING OLD TELEPHONES OR EVEN STUDYING ABOUT THE CIVIL WAR...THIS IS CALLED, "PLAYING WITH THE PAST"

REALLY? CERTAINLY!!! AND THIS IS GOOD FOR IT HELPS THESE MEN TO COPE WITH THEIR EVERYDAY PROBLEMS...

NOW, I FEEL THAT IT IS ABSOLUTELY NECESSARY FOR ME TO GET MY BLANKET BACK SO I'M JUST GOING TO GIVE IT A GOOD...

..YANK!

IT'S SURPRISING WHAT YOU CAN ACCOMPLISH WITH A LITTLE SMOOTH TALKING AND SOME FAST ACTION!

SCHULZ

FASCINATING.. COMPLETELY FASCINATING..

SEE THAT GROUP OF STARS, SALLY?

THAT'S CALLED THE "BIG DIPPER"

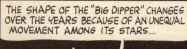

THE SHAPE OF THE "BIG DIPPER" CHANGES OVER THE YEARS BECAUSE OF AN UNEQUAL MOVEMENT AMONG ITS STARS...

IN ANOTHER HUNDRED THOUSAND YEARS THE "BIG DIPPER" WILL BE GONE..

~WAAH!~

SCHULZ

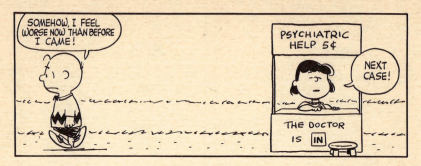

AAUGH!

HOW DOES HE **KNOW**? HOW DOES HE **DO** IT?!!!

HOW DID HE KNOW I HAD A COOKIE IN MY POCKET WHEN I WENT BY HIM THE SECOND TIME?

HE LISTENS TO YOUR FOOTSTEPS.. WITH THE COOKIE IN YOUR POCKET, YOU **WEIGHED** MORE!

THE ONLY WAY YOU CAN SURVIVE THESE DAYS IS TO KEEP YOUR EAR TO THE GROUND!

TIME OUT!

I GOTTA HAVE A LITTLE CONFERENCE WITH OUR PITCHER-MANAGER.. A BASEBALL GAME IS NOTHING WITHOUT A FEW CONFERENCES...

WELL, MANAGER, HOW'S THE GAME GOING? EVERYTHING OKAY HERE ON THE PITCHER'S MOUND?

I'M ALWAYS AMAZED AT HOW FAR YOU CAN SEE FROM UP HERE... WE DON'T GET ANY SORT OF VIEW AT ALL FROM THE OUTFIELD...

GEE...I'LL BET YOU COULD EVEN SLIDE DOWN THIS THING IF YOU WANTED TO...SURE, YOU CAN..SEE?

LOOK OUT! HERE I COME!

WHEEEEEEE

LOOK OUT! HERE I COME AGAIN!

GET OUT OF HERE!

CHARLIE BROWN WILL NEVER MAKE A GOOD MANAGER...HE'S TOO CRABBY!

SCHULZ

THE EARLY MORNING LIGHT REVEALS A VULTURE PERCHED HIGH ON THE LIMB OF A TREE

AH! A VICTIM!

THE VULTURE PEERS...

HE SWOOPS!

BONG!

RATS! HOW HUMILIATING!

A GOOD VULTURE HATES TO ACCEPT CHARITY!

I SUPPOSE IF I TOLD YOU THERE'S A VULTURE OUTSIDE THAT'S BOTHERING ME, YOU'D SAY I WAS CRAZY, WOULDN'T YOU?

YES, I WOULD!

WHAT HAPPENED TO YOUR VULTURE?

HE'S NOT BOTHERING ME ANY MORE...HE GOT TREE SICK!

FORGET IT.... IT WAS A HOME RUN!

CAN I HELP IT IF MY HOUSE FACES THE BALL PARK?

"WHEN SHE SAW THE LITTLE HOUSE IN THE WOODS, SHE WONDERED WHO LIVED THERE SO SHE KNOCKED AT THE DOOR. NO ONE ANSWERED SO SHE KNOCKED AGAIN."

WHAT DO YOU THINK WILL HAPPEN?

I CAN'T IMAGINE

"...STILL NO ONE ANSWERED, SO GOLDILOCKS OPENED THE DOOR AND WALKED IN. THERE BEFORE HER, IN THE LITTLE ROOM, SHE SAW A TABLE SET FOR THREE..."

"THERE WAS A GREAT BIG BOWL OF PORRIDGE, A MIDDLE-SIZED BOWL OF PORRIDGE, AND A LITTLE, WEE BOWL OF PORRIDGE. SHE TASTED THE GREAT BIG BOWL OF PORRIDGE..."

"'OH, THIS IS TOO HOT,' SHE SAID. THEN SHE TASTED THE MIDDLE-SIZED BOWL OF PORRIDGE. 'OH, THIS IS TOO COLD.' THEN SHE TASTED THE LITTLE, WEE BOWL. 'OH, THIS IS JUST RIGHT,' SHE SAID, AND SHE ATE IT ALL UP.'"

I HAVE A QUESTION!

ABOUT WHAT?

WELL, IT'S IN REGARD TO COOLING... IT WOULD SEEM TO ME THAT IF THE MIDDLE-SIZED BOWL WAS COLD, THE LITTLE, WEE BOWL WOULD BE COLD, TOO, RATHER THAN 'JUST RIGHT,' AND..

POW!

I NEVER EVEN BROUGHT UP THE FAR MORE OBVIOUS POINT OF UNLAWFUL ENTRY!

TODAY IS BEETHOVEN'S BIRTHDAY!

HAPPY BIRTHDAY TO YOU.... HAPPY BIRTHDAY TO YOU....

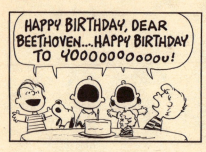

HAPPY BIRTHDAY, DEAR BEETHOVEN....HAPPY BIRTHDAY TO YOOOOOOoooU!

CUT THE CAKE! CUT THE CAKE!

WHAT A PARTY! ISN'T THIS GREAT?

THIS HAS BEEN THE BEST BEETHOVEN'S BIRTHDAY PARTY EVER!

I LIKED THE PART WHERE WE LISTENED TO THE FINALE OF THE NINTH SYMPHONY...

OH, FREUNDE, NICHT DIESE TÖNE!

GREAT! GREAT! JUST GREAT!

WELL, THANKS FOR COMING...I'M GLAD YOU ENJOYED YOURSELVES..

WE'LL BE BACK NEXT YEAR!

NOW THAT EVERYONE HAS GONE, I'D LIKE TO ASK YOU SOMETHING, SCHROEDER

WHO WAS BEETHOVEN?

OH, NO!
NOT AGAIN!

WHAT IN THE WORLD IS THE MATTER WITH YOU?

I'M AWARE OF MY TONGUE!

YOU'RE WHAT?!

I'M AWARE OF MY TONGUE...

IT'S AN AWFUL FEELING! EVERY NOW AND THEN I BECOME AWARE THAT I HAVE A TONGUE INSIDE MY MOUTH, AND THEN IT STARTS TO FEEL ALL LUMPED UP...

THAT'S THE MOST STUPID THING I'VE EVER HEARD!

I CAN'T HELP IT...I CAN'T PUT IT OUT OF MY MIND...I KEEP THINKING ABOUT WHERE MY TONGUE WOULD BE IF I WEREN'T THINKING ABOUT IT AND THEN I CAN FEEL IT SORT OF PRESSING AGAINST MY TEETH...

NOW IT FEELS ALL LUMPED UP AGAIN.. THE MORE I TRY TO PUT IT OUT OF MY MIND, THE MORE I THINK ABOUT IT...

GOOD GRIEF!

!

OH, NO!!

I OUGHTA KNOCK YOUR BLOCK OFF!

SCHROEDER, WHAT IF YOU AND I WERE TO GET MARRIED SOME DAY, AND WHAT IF WE..

I CAN'T COMPREHEND WHAT YOU'RE SAYING

WELL, WHAT I MEAN IS, IF YOU AND I EVER GET MARRIED, WILL ...

NO, I CAN'T COMPREHEND THAT... I CAN'T CONCEIVE THAT EVER HAPPENING..

WELL, LET'S JUST SAY IT DID, AND...

NO, I JUST CAN'T CONCEIVE OF SUCH A THING.. IT'S LIKE THINKING ABOUT WHAT LIES BEYOND OUTER SPACE..MY MIND CAN'T COMPREHEND THAT...

BUT CAN'T WE JUST SAY THAT BY SOME MIRACLE WE DID GET MARRIED, AND...

NO, MY MIND CANNOT EVEN BEGIN TO GRASP SUCH A THOUGHT...IT REELS... THE WHOLE CONCEPT IS SIMPLY BEYOND MY COMPREHENSION

MY AUNT MARIAN WAS RIGHT... NEVER TRY TO DISCUSS MARRIAGE WITH A MUSICIAN !

PAT PAT PAT

YOUR BROTHER PATS BIRDS ON THE HEAD..

WHAT?

ARE YOU OUT OF YOUR MIND?!

ARE YOU TRYING TO MAKE US THE LAUGHING STOCK OF THE WHOLE COMMUNITY'?

HOW LONG DO YOU THINK WE'LL LAST AROUND HERE IF WORD GETS OUT THAT YOU PAT BIRDS ON THE HEAD?

NOW, CUT IT OUT!!

HOW ABOUT DOGS?

DOGS ARE ALL RIGHT...YOU CAN PAT ALL THE DOGS YOU WANT.. IN FACT, SOCIETY APPROVES OF PATTING DOGS ON THE HEAD!

THERE ARE MANY THINGS I DON'T UNDERSTAND..

SIGH

HOLD STILL!

HOLD STILL, I SAY!

IS THIS A SCHOOL PROJECT, LUCY?

OF COURSE, IT IS, YOU BLOCKHEAD! WHY ELSE WOULD I BE CHASING A BUNCH OF STUPID BUTTERFLIES?!

HERE... I THINK MAYBE YOUR TEACHER WILL LIKE THESE..

PROMISE YOU'LL LET THEM GO AFTER YOU'VE STUDIED THEM, WILL YOU?

I JUST CAN'T BELIEVE THAT RACHEL CARSON WOULD EVER LET HERSELF GET SO UPSET!